LAUNCHING A
Career in Philanthropy

PRACTICES OF HIGHLY EFFECTIVE FUNDRAISERS

HARVEY GREEN, FAHP, CFRE

Ordering Information:
For details, contact Harveyg3@aol.com

Print ISBN: 978-1-09835-951-5
eBook ISBN: 978-1-09835-952-2

Printed in the United States of America on SFI Certified paper.

First Edition

TABLE OF CONTENTS

Part III

ACKNOWLEDGMENTS

First and foremost, I would like to thank my family: my wife, Joan and my two daughters, Jada and Carly. Without them, this book would not have been possible. When I talk to my children, I am reminded of what it means to be uninhibited by the limiting beliefs that are imposed on us as adults. It's amazing to recognize that when children believe they can do anything, they stop at nothing and pursue their destinations with relentless optimism. Ironically, we as adults should mirror their attitudes and have the dreams, drive, and energy that children do. There's a quote by Marianne Williamson in her book *A Return to Love* that reads: "Our deepest fear is not that we are inadequate. Our deepest fear is that we are powerful beyond measure. It is our light, not our darkness that most frightens us. We ask ourselves, who am I to be brilliant, gorgeous, talented, and fabulous? Actually, who are you *not* to be?" This is one of the most powerful quotes that I have ever read in my life—I believe it speaks to our ordained ability to do what we were meant to do in life, regardless of our backgrounds and circumstances. Most importantly, if we set our minds on doing something—whether in business, in our personal lives, or in fundraising—we have an innate ability to achieve a level of excellence. This is an important point for you to acknowledge as you look to grow in the fundraising profession. It will serve you well and you will accomplish things that you never thought were possible—beyond raising large sums of money—you will have a tremendous impact on the organizations that you work for.

I'd like to think that I have managed to write this book from my own brain, but the truth is, a lot of people contributed, and I am thankful for their professional opinions. So, I'd like to explicitly thank the following for helping me to piece this book together: Jim Husson, Liz Shear, Kate Carinder and Leslie Chambers. Thanks to the countless number of colleagues whom I've had the pleasure to work with throughout the course of my career. You have all played an instrumental part in helping me to attain success in this field!

INTRODUCTION—

How a tattered business card and a stack of blankets changed my life.

On an unseasonably warm spring day, I anxiously waded through morning rush hour traffic in Los Angeles, California. Two things crossed my mind. One, that I drank too much water during my morning workout, and two, that I needed to find a bathroom fast! I try to live a life of being well hydrated, but on that day I wished I had taken a detour from my health regimen. Needless to say, I was in a state of nervous agitation and was far from the mindset I needed to be in for what was about to happen. As I navigated to my destination, I remember nervously looking down at my GPS as the estimated arrival time continued to increase while traffic thickened. The dreadful thought of feeling lost ensued, and I was certain that I would be late for my big meeting. I was in search of the location for my final interview with James "Jim"

Husson, the senior vice president of the sophisticated advancement operation at Boston College and one of the most articulate and successful fundraisers in higher education. In distracted thought, I was trying to rehearse what I was going to say to Jim during my interview but was simultaneously jaded with negative thoughts and feelings. Thoughts of not being "good enough" entered my mind, and I began to question whether I had what it took to enter the development ranks. Although my background of being commissioned as an officer in the Marine Corps, serving as a federal business manager for a Fortune 500 company, and owning and operating my own personal training business had given me important skill sets, I still carried an unfounded doubt. I was taught the value of leadership, relationship building and felt like I knew how to close "deals." Aware of the fundamental principles of business in the private sector left me at a loss in the nonprofit industry. As far as I was concerned, I was very much a "newbie" in this industry, and these thoughts gave me anxiety about my upcoming meeting with Jim.

I realized that I needed to gain focus for what was about to come. Alas, I found the location of my meeting, took care of "business," and I began to think about my conversation with Jim. What Jim didn't know was that I had previously visited the campus of Boston College (BC)—I am married to an alumna—and that I had the chance to walk across campus and enjoy the scenes of what is aptly known as the "Heights", the center and focal point of the

2

university. On my trip there, I also had the chance to stop by the fundraising office, which they call the Office of Advancement, to conduct my own personal reconnaissance mission. I visualized working there and realized that this opportunity would be the culmination of all my professional experiences. To me, the conscious choice to work at BC was in complete alignment with what I valued on a personal level.

While on my mission, I had a visual recollection of my role model, a guidance counselor from my hometown in inner-city Miami whose words affected me deeply as a high school student. I recalled a day when Ms. Betty Gunshor took me under her wing when I was facing many difficult personal, family, and financial challenges. On one memorable day, Ms. Gunshor looked me square in the eyes and said, "Harvey Green, whatever you decide to do in your life, you can, in fact, do it. All you have to do is make the choice." Now, Ms. Gunshor did not know me much better than any of the other 700-plus rising seniors who attended Hialeah Miami Lakes High School, but somehow she knew through the great difficulty that I was facing in my personal and family situation, I also had the power to persevere and to succeed in anything I thought to be possible. Ms. Gunshor knew of my long days of catching a city bus to a school bus stop so I could continue to go to the same high school with my friends. I recall when our family lost our home, I would stay late at the library so I had additional time to not only study, but figure out where I was going to sleep. The extra time I spent studying paid off, because I became a straight "A" student. It still brings tears to my eyes to think that Ms. Gunshor helped me to get into college at the University of Florida by not only her profound encouragement, but by also supplying me with pillows, sheets and blankets for my dorm room. I knew that through personal perseverance, the facilitation of a few resources and the blessings of God, I was an empowered person who was destined to do great things. The power of Ms. Gunshor's philanthropy and kindness has positively impacted my life in so many ways. It propelled me from growing up as a child in inner-city Miami, to receiving a scholarship, to becoming someone capable of accomplishing anything I set my mind to. To me, the job that I was interviewing for with Jim was a way to pay it forward. I genuinely felt that a career in philanthropy could help other students who walked in the same footsteps as me. I knew I wanted to be that vital conduit between the donors and the institution to help students secure their futures through education. For me, making all of these points were important to emphasize in my interview with Jim.

I managed to pull it all together for my conversation with Jim. His affable nature put me at ease, and I felt that I was handling his questions well. As things were starting to wrap up, I realized that I had one more secret weapon. On my previous reconnaissance mission to BC, I secured a business card that was on the front desk of the Advancement Office. I had written on the back of it,

"**I WILL WORK HERE.**" I put that card in my wallet and carried it around for one year. At the moment of truth when Jim and I were wrapping up our interview, he posed one last question to me. He asked, "Harvey, what separates you from other candidates who already have relevant fundraising experience?". I knew at that moment that I had to go for broke and that if I really wanted to break into this industry, I was going to have to take a leap of faith. I reached down in my pocket for my wallet and pulled out a tattered business card that read, "Boston College Office of Advancement" on the front. I held it up to Jim's curious eyes and started to tell him about my past travels to BC, my commitment to what this industry represents, and how the ideals of his organization resonated with me personally. I told him that I had made a personal commitment to excellence in this industry and how the very essence of what philanthropy represents made me who I am in life. As I said all of this, I turned over the business card that read, "**I WILL WORK HERE**" and explained to Jim my story of carrying the card around for one year in anticipation of this moment. This story somehow preceded my arrival to Boston College and marked the beginning of my life as a full-fledged fundraiser. So, it begins there.

WHO IS THIS BOOK FOR?

It is my hope that this book can serve as a compelling testament to how a personal story and a strong desire can help you achieve success as a fundraiser. Jim Husson served as a great mentor to me, and I must say that there have been many along the way. My wife Joan has been my biggest fan and has always pushed me to be a better version of myself. I remember after I sold my personal training business in southern California, I was convinced that the right career path would automatically "jump out at me." Well, after months on end, it did not—but then, on one auspicious evening, as my wife and I watched a *60 Minutes* episode about the establishment of a New York nonprofit, I had an epiphany and I knew that this was the industry for me. Geoffrey Canada, former CEO of the Harlem Children's Zone (HCZ), an inner-city charter school, was being featured in what made for quite an amazing story. It basically talked about how Mr. Canada and his team at the HCZ were literally changing the lives of hundreds, if not thousands, of children—their mission was to educate and increase high school graduation rates among students in Harlem. His model has become a national one and a beacon of hope to many including Former President Barack Obama who suggested in a news article that projects like the HCZ should be started all over the country. A huge part of Mr. Canada's role was to cultivate and inspire potential donors who would be passionate about the vision of HCZ. His list included many of the big names we know in modern day philanthropy. Mr. Canada's promise of getting underprivileged kids through school creates real and permanent change in the world. It is a vision that has impacted the lives of many. When I saw Mr. Canada on that show—I realized that I too wanted the responsibility of helping to educate students who clearly had the talent and the smarts, but lacked the resources to attend high schools and colleges that will furnish them with a better opportunity to succeed in life. I am so inspired by people doing work like Mr. Canada, and his story and professional experiences helped motivate me to pursue a career in fundraising.

My hope is that this book inspires a few audiences. It is for those who are contemplating entering fundraising as a profession, as well as those who are already in the industry and want to take their careers to a new level. In the chapters that follow, I will briefly speak about the origins of development and philanthropy, the value of having a personal philosophy, and behaviors that I have observed from some of the most highly effective fundraisers. In the second part of the book, I will cover some of the most remarkable personal habits of highly effective fundraisers, learn about what makes a highly effective fundraiser from a donor's perspective, and examine challenges that fundraisers face and how to overcome them. In the last part of this book, we will look at some ways that highly effective fundraisers motivate themselves and win every time, segue into a brief discussion about becoming a leader in this industry, and conclude with some practical tips on making a successful fundraising career happen.

Former CEO of the Harlem Children's Zone in New York, Geoffrey Canada responded to a letter I sent him about fundraising. "Harvey, stay on this path, it will bring you rich rewards." As Mr. Canada inspired me, I want to inspire you on how to grow your career in fundraising. You can achieve personal and financial success while at the same time fulfilling your great social obligation as a human being in this field. I have always thought that you should have three things in life: professional goals, family goals, and social goals, and that success in one of these areas does not guarantee success in all of them. I feel that a career in fundraising is a way to fulfill those three buckets.

Quick disclaimer. By no means is this meant to be an exhaustive book of all things fundraising, nor am I claiming to be an expert. This book relays the culmination of my experiences as a fundraiser and the observations that I have made along the way. There are many fundraisers out there doing some very impactful things and are experiencing massive success. It is my hope that this book gives you a little insight into the formula of that success.

PART I

CHAPTER 1:

The Scope of the Industry

Evolution of Philanthropy

This section is by no means an exhaustive historical account of philanthropy. However, I think it is important for you to have some insight into the background of this industry. Philanthropy and its application through "fundraising" essentially started when this country was formed. From the dawn of medieval times in the 14th and 15th centuries to the tyranny of feudalism and its collapse, philanthropy paved the way for urban life. Through the aftermath of conflict, war, and tension, early societies recognized they needed to rebuild by forming stronger communities—hence the ideas for addressing these needs through philanthropy began to emerge. In the post-Revolutionary War era, the effects of the Industrial Revolution brought about major changes in American life. These changes charged the early shapers to consider what it meant to be a free nation and how philanthropy could help citizens attain and solidify their position in the world. With the idea of being a free and independent nation, many early influencers thought of ways to help protect and serve the human condition.

In the 19th century, philanthropists began to respond to immediate social needs. Individuals such as Andrew Carnegie, who had ideas about distributing wealth for public good, had a dramatic effect on education, culture, science, and public health. His ideas began to spread worldwide, and he inspired many others to follow his lead. This early momentum was the catalyst in essentially paving the way into what we have today. We find that, through our current practice of philanthropy and the constant way that we evolve to meet the growing needs in society, we remain true to the great philanthropic traditions of the past. We know philanthropy today is more organized, sophisticated, and global than ever before. Philanthropists have become savvier and constantly strive to find innovative and creative ways to work with nonprofits for a wide variety of causes. Whether they are helping to improve and strengthen communities, promoting the arts, building schools, combating public epidemics, or providing relief for the victims of war and natural disasters, philanthropists have been involved like never before. The level of engagement of philanthropists who have been active locally, nationally, and globally is unprecedented. According to the nonprofit resource *Giving*

USA, the number of hours that volunteers help organizations is at an all-time high, and we know that giving from individuals is the single largest form of philanthropic support. In my opinion, now is the right time to be a part of this profession—even though we find ourselves amid the COVID-19 global pandemic.

The Vast Nonprofit Industry

Data from one of the philanthropic sector's foremost publications, *The Chronicle of Philanthropy*, suggests that there are well over 1.5 million charities and foundations in the United States alone. These nonprofits consist of educational institutions, health care organizations, relief and aid organizations, museums, and institutions of art, to name just a few. They all have one thing in common—they are in need of raising money and are fiercely competing for donors—individuals and private foundations who can, in a sense, help them accomplish their missions. These nonprofits need skilled and competent professionals from a variety of backgrounds to help them go out and champion their message. They are looking for people who can persuade, influence, and inspire others not only to be engaged with the organization on a volunteer level, but also to dedicate resources, primarily financial, to support their distinct causes. This financial support can take the forms of cash, pledges, appreciated stocks, real estate, and in many instances, bequests or estate gifts.

Given the shifting national demographics of our nation, I am finding that the professional backgrounds of today's fundraisers are numerous. This industry has become much more sophisticated in that we now have development professionals equipped with PhDs, MAs, and JDs. Additionally, many people who now work with nonprofit organizations or seek employment in this arena come from industries where their transferable skills are highly useful. They infuse a unique diversity into today's organizations. I have seen people who have attained a fair amount of success who have hailed from the financial sector—areas such as banking or real estate and investment fund management—to professionals who have led careers in the sales and service industries. The good news in this industry is that a variety of backgrounds are welcomed, and the fundamental ability to understand business, coupled with a relentless drive to be an asset to an organization's mission are highly desirable traits. This news should bring you encouragement if you are looking to transition into fundraising. Overall, we can predict that the vastness of this profession will continue to grow and be able to meet the evolving needs of sophisticated donors.

Competition for Talent

The growth of the fundraising profession will naturally create competition across different nonprofit organizations. With an influx of professionals with diversified skill sets, competition to recruit and retain the best and the brightest of this talent will be prevalent. I have seen development professionals recruited away for upwards 40% or more of their current salaries, and in many times, to locations that are right across the street. There are roughly more than 1.5 million nonprofit organizations that are eagerly on the beat in search for the right talent to help garner philanthropic support. Organizations can go through somewhat of a tumultuous and expensive process of finding the most qualified fundraising professionals, and in many cases, these searches fail. There is a statistic that, for every marketable fundraiser, there are about six to eight jobs available in the nonprofit sector—talk about competition! The search for talent has really become an arms race, and we are seeing recruiting and consulting firms busy tending to massive talent pool management. So, the bottom line is this, I feel that this is a buyers' market for fundraisers, which is encouraging from a job security standpoint. However, how will fundraisers differentiate themselves from the competition and experience a great deal of success in this profession? These are questions that I will address later on in this book.

The Flip Side: High Turnover Rates

The expected dilemma that organizations are coping with, as they rush to secure the best and the brightest talent, is turnover.

I have found that sometimes the industry moves way too fast in trying to recruit talent because of the fierce competition. Many times, organizations make decisions to hire candidates out of sheer desperation or panic, and do not take the time to appropriately vet out or properly assess the talent that they truly need. I have witnessed an organization after the hiring process realize that the candidate they selected did not have the right skills, abilities, and knowledge to do the job—and had to take steps to part ways. Amazingly, some of these basic things, such as having the right skills, do not even come out in the interview process in some unscrupulous organizations. I have seen new hires frustratingly "tap out" upon finding that the leadership or the culture of their recently joined organization is dysfunctional, or because they have not been given clear direction on their responsibilities. Not only is this frustrating on both sides, it is a precious waste of time and resources. Before you know it, both parties can end up back at the drawing board. So, if you are new to this field or are transitioning, make sure that you are taking an educated approach and find out all you can about a prospective employer. Take the time to "look under the hood" and ask the really hard questions, as you deem appropriate, in your interview process. Remember, you are interviewing them as well! Lastly, do your best to resist the allure of huge salaries and big titles as primary motivations in your search. I have found that those with this approach have ventured down this road unsuccessfully. Don't get me wrong, money and titles are important, but be sure you lend as much attention to the mission and the culture of your perspective employer. I feel that if these things are in alignment, then the money and titles will eventually follow. As I mentioned above—there is an abundance of opportunities for talented fundraisers, so you will have the chance to choose the organization that is the best fit for you. I would recommend that you find a place where you can be really passionate about the organization's direction and leadership, then claim your stake. If you perform well and stick through some of the inevitable periods of ups and downs, you will undoubtedly rise within the organization. I have seen examples in organizations where a candidate started out in an administrative support role and, over the years, progressed to the ranks of higher leadership. You will find that with a little bit of patience and perseverance, you will do great things for your organization and have the ability to have a positive impact.

CHAPTER 2:

Personal Philosophies of Highly Effective Fundraisers

Have a Why

Here is where we start to delve into the heart of highly effective fundraisers. Considering the robust history of philanthropy that I outlined in chapter one, some fundraisers at best tend to tell a mediocre story of why they chose this profession as a career. When asked, some people relate the message that, by happenstance, they simply "fell into" fundraising. As a manager and as someone who takes this field to heart, this implies that their actions were not purposeful, or well thought out. Furthermore, I have noticed through conducting hundreds of interviews and having worked with many fundraisers throughout my career, that this tentative mentality short-circuits longevity and success. I am a firm believer in the fact that if you don't have a true passion for what you're doing—and are unaware of your "why" for doing it—it will be hard to be as successful at being one of the best. I would encourage you as a fundraiser to always know your "why." I've kept in touch with Jim Husson, the senior vice president for the Office of Advancement at Boston College about this subject. He mentioned that highly effective fundraisers should have three things: 1) a hyper-focus on their institution; 2) a personal passion for philanthropy; and 3) a personal deep-down conviction for what they do every day. He said that he's seen fundraisers start at the same point in time in their careers and would analyze their respective progress three years out. He realized that, if we made all things equal, such as a fundraiser's assignments, portfolios, and territories, there will always be a substantial performance edge between the fundraiser who has these three things in check versus the fundraisers who are missing one or more of these key qualities.

What folks like Jim and other development professionals know is that you must have a solid "why" and a passion for getting into this business. I encourage you to find the story of why you do what you do. A story that you can define so well that the very thought of it infuses enthusiasm in how you go about your job every day. Trust me, your donors and prospects and supervisors will know if your "heart" is into what you do. You will find that, in conversations with people you meet with, the subject of why you fundraise for your institution will inevitably come up and you should be prepared with a solid and compelling answer. Although in most of your meetings with prospects, you will make full use of the 80/20 rule—that is, you do 20% of the talking and dedicate 80% to listening and responding to their needs—always be prepared to answer a few personal questions as you build rapport. Also remember, always allow your prospect the space to tell their story as well; it is a great way to learn more about what fuels their interests. You can take the conversation further by asking well-thought-out and open-ended questions that deal directly with the information that they are saying to you at that given moment. You will find that because you so eloquently articulated your "whys" earlier in the conversation, you will have put the donor at ease because they feel that they are speaking with someone who is in alignment with their passions and the things that are most meaningful to them. It's simply the law of reciprocation at work. Through knowing your "why," a fundraiser will be able to form good relationships with prospects and donors as well as help them uncover their philanthropic desires more effectively. So, don't be afraid to show your enthusiasm as well as explore shared passions with your prospect—you will find that you are able to form strong relationships.

Philanthropy: "Love of Humanity"

As you begin to work on your personal story and philosophy on why you work in this field, there are some other important concepts to grasp. Philanthropy, by its very definition is a word derived from the ancient Greek meaning, "love of humanity." As was mentioned earlier, philanthropy is thought of as being a solution to some of society's most pressing problems and has been a vehicle for discovering some of the root causes of many challenges we face worldwide. Furthermore, we know that the giving of financial resources and the donation of volunteer time and expertise are some of the ways that people can be philanthropic. The impact of all of this and what philanthropy can do to change lives is profound. When you have the tremendous responsibility of being a fundraiser for your organization, keep these important concepts in mind and know that the change that you help create in your role is very important. Weave these broader themes of what philanthropy has the power to achieve into your own personal story to make what you do more real. I am sure that if you really think hard about some of the opportunities that you were given in life, you'd be able to uncover a story that ties directly into philanthropy. I bet that, through this process of soul searching, you will get a stronger sense of gratitude for all the things you have in your life, which will empower you to be a highly effective fundraiser.

Alignment with the Mission

Many nonprofits set out to do great things in society—everything from saving the whales to helping to discover a cure for cancer to protecting against the abuse of animals, educating students and providing humanitarian assistance and relief from natural disasters. There is an endless amount of need out there, and an endless number of things that organizations want to accomplish in accordance with their mission. For those of you who are new to fundraising, be sure you do the necessary research on organizations whose missions personally resonate with you. Before applying for a position, be sure to read over the organization's mission statement—much of this information can be found on their website or by accessing some of their 990 information. A 990 is an informational tax form that most tax-exempt organizations must file annually to the IRS that gives an overview of the organization's activities, governance, and financial information. You can also find information in an organization's annual report, which not only gives you information on the scope of the organization's work, but also presents a fundraising report that may highlight donor and volunteer-related activities. At times, these reports can tell you if the institution is amid a big campaign, has successfully closed a campaign, or perhaps is getting ready to go into a campaign. Campaigns are huge fundraising drivers for an organization as they look to create public awareness around their priorities as well as any distinguished programs or initiatives that they hope to bring to fruition. These can range from the creation of new buildings, programs, or perhaps endowments for research and other specialized projects. The point is to do your homework thoroughly and make sure you solidly know what you seek in the way of employment at your prospective nonprofit. The aforementioned documents will give you a pretty good picture of where an organization is, as well as what some of the challenges may be. After conducting this process of doing your own due diligence, you should feel comfortable in applying to the respective organizations that 1.) meet your personal standards, 2.) give you confidence in their direction, and 3.) have a strong connection to your own personal story or "why."

New to the Field? Choose Wisely

You have control of the steering wheel in your career as a fundraiser. Take your time and make the right choices for you. We all know that salary, location, and benefits are important and relevant to any job. However, I encourage you to do the necessary research on the places you'd like to raise money for—this will save you a lot of time and headaches. Remember that you have the power to create the career that you want to lead. As a reminder, don't fall into the trap of thinking that you must have a big title or the feeling that you must work for a huge institution. If you are highly effective at your job in a place that you can be the most passionate about—the grandest of things will eventually happen in your career. So, are you excited?!

CHAPTER 3:

Behaviors of Highly Effective Fundraisers

Commitment to Greatness

In the previous chapter, I emphasized how important it is to have a strong resonance to the mission of the nonprofit that you are fundraising for. However, your own personal commitment to success in your role will make a tremendous difference. You can ask any respectable fundraiser, and they will tell you that development jobs are not for the faint-hearted. Unlike in the mostly straightforward sales industry in the private sector, development jobs require a remarkably different skill set. The process of identifying prospects, meeting with them, and developing a relationship with them for a period of 12–18 months—yes, it takes that long to secure a significant gift—requires today's fundraising professional to have a diverse skill set. A fundraising professional has to be adept at having the proper tactfulness to discuss personal matters of philanthropy with respective prospects, be able to employ creative and strategic thinking in their work, and lastly have an incredible amount of patience to go through the process. I have noticed that the process of fundraising is almost like solving a puzzle where you are strategically trying to put the smaller pieces together to form the big picture of where you see the prospective donor and organization's needs fulfilled. It takes the sharpest of investigative skills—not that we are FBI agents or anything of the sort—as well as wit, creativity, and a tenacity as in no other profession that I have seen. You are put into an arena with smart, savvy, and devoted people who want to make a difference and will expect nothing less than your "A" game. Most of all, you have to be bold and sometimes take calculated risks when you have to make "the ask" for money. This is the true test of any fundraiser. Once you know the feeling of having to make "the ask" once, it is an exhilarating feeling that you will constantly crave and always seek, particularly if you have been successful in getting a "yes"! However, note that even some of the best fundraisers have been turned down for a variety of reasons and that rejection by no means should be taken personally. These fundraisers know that each "no" they've received in their careers has brought them closer to a "yes" and that temporary setbacks are a natural part of the business. Having the strength and tenacity to endure the ups and downs of this type of work will most definitely require a strong will on your part. When you find yourself deep in the trenches, remember to fall back on your "why" and reaffirm your commitment to this profession. Get ready because you will get denied and rejected, and some people won't even take your phone calls. You'd have to realize that, in many cases, success will come down to the right timing and the fact that fundraising can be a numbers game—the more people you reach out to, the greater your chances for success. So, stay committed!

Higher Level of Self-Awareness

In finding donors to support our organizations, we in fundraising metaphorically say that we "kiss many frogs" in search for that desired "prince" or "princess." Through what can be an arduous prospect discovery process, it is important that you maintain a higher level of self- awareness in your thoughts, habits and the way you go about implementing your strategies. This higher level of awareness is the ability to keep your daily focus on how you can have a real impact on your organization and the people it serves. With this mindset, you will find yourself undeterred by setbacks, minutiae, and potential dysfunction that may exist within your organization. Yes, there can be some dysfunction! So, remember to always hone in on the things that you can immediately control and things that only propel you forward in your job as a fundraiser. You will have to know from a place inside of you that this is what you were designed to do and that, if you persevere, you will have long-term success in this industry. If you are reading this book, I believe that you have been called to do this great work and that if you focus on what initially lured you into this field, your day-to-day work will be above board. You will find that there may be days of disappointment due to rejection from prospects, your peers, or maybe your supervisors, but always keep the highest version of yourself in mind. This idea makes for some of the greatest qualities of highly effective fundraisers—they know what their purpose is, and they know what they are capable of achieving. These higher thoughts drive their everyday actions. It is almost as if they are in a "fundraising zone"—I invite you to be a part of this zone.

Perceptive Power

I certainly don't mean to be too "Zen-like" in this section, although I am a big fan of a more enlightened way of thinking. What I've come to notice is that many highly effective fundraisers I have met in this industry possess an uncanny ability to efficiently size up situations and produce thoughtful actions. In the midst of their work, whether with a prospect, making a strategic decision, or leading a team, they somehow always find the right things to do in any given situation. I have noticed this skill is acquired from past experiences in their fundraising careers combined with their ability to trust their natural instincts. They instinctively know how to enter a room with grace and find the right connectors and people to speak to. In many high-stakes situations, they know how to consciously and relentlessly move their organization's mission forward. Somehow, their "magnet" attracts the right people at the right time, and they know how to put themselves in a situation where development magic happens. I believe that some people possess these abilities innately, but I am of the school of thought that this skill can be learned by watching some of the best in this field. It's just a matter of fine-tuning your development antenna. It takes time to develop the perceptive power that many fundraisers have—so be patient with yourself as you tune your antenna. With hard work, patience, and tenacity, you will most certainly become a fundraising professional who has the ability to part a room like the Red Sea and be known in this industry as a rainmaker. I've seen highly effective fundraisers defy the typical fundraising cycles (it is said that it traditionally takes 12-18 months to successfully close a significant gift) and inspire swift donor action. It will take time to develop your perceptive power, and you will need to build up an abundance of trust with your donors to get to this level. However, once you develop this power, you will gain a tremendous amount of professional respect in your field and will do everything short of levitation!

Overcoming Challenges

You will find that the dynamic and exciting life of a fundraiser is an adventure every day. You will fire on all your cylinders and have some major wins on some days, but on other days, you will not. It is the nature of this beast, and you will have to find a way to turn your challenges into opportunities. I can't tell you how many times that I have failed to meet the mark. I recall many times being prepared for a big solicitation that I thought would certainly be funded by a prospect end up in a crash and burn. This may seem unfortunate, but I have learned to interpret these experiences in a different way. Failure will in fact happen, but the good news is that these failures teach us very valuable lessons. Fortunately for those in this profession, there are many generous and philanthropic individuals out there, so there will always be hope for another chance to be successful. And, the fact of the matter is this, our experiences—good or bad—teach us valuable lessons that prepare us for future encounters with prospective donors. One of the main challenges that I needed to overcome to be a better development professional was to change my personal thoughts about money. Growing up where I'm from, inner city Miami, the idea of giving away money to anyone, let alone any organization, was foreign. I grew up with a different mentality about what money meant and was ingrained with the ideals that money was scarce and that if you got too much of it, you were somehow "evil." In my local church, the principle of tithing or giving 10% of your income was encouraged, but my family did not consistently adhere to this practice. These old thoughts and ideas followed me throughout life and made me very apprehensive about handling money and making money, let alone asking for it. As I became college educated and had the chance to experience life in the private sector, I began to embrace what philanthropy truly is, and my paradigms about money began to shift. I also thought about the impact that philanthropy had on my own life, the reasons behind why people give, and the impact that generous donors can have on the world. Additionally, I finally realized that I was in control of my thoughts of what the power of money could accomplish and realized that money, while it can be used for evil, is an effective vehicle in helping to make positive change in the world and that money that is available to the universe is in abundance. I had to consciously throw out my old ideas about money, and as I began to develop stronger, more empowering ideas, I developed a habit of constantly thinking that my place in the world as a fundraiser can be used to help channel wealth toward the greater good. The idea of asking for money is not about you or me personally—it is about humanity and all that can be accomplished by those who have the resources and willingness to give to the plethora of needs out there. A fundraiser's job comes down to this: we are the vital conduits bridging those who have a desire to make a difference with those in need of real and sustainable change. When you think of it like that, you again understand the importance of your role as a fundraiser. Realizing that I am a facilitator in this dynamic world of philanthropy and that "the ask" is not about me, allows me to take the pressure off when I ask a prospect for money. It is truly about the mission of the organization. I remember my first ask as a young development officer on a visit to Houston, Texas, in the middle of the summer. The prospect was a prominent attorney, "Sue," who was working as a partner at a mid-sized firm. She had received the benefit of scholarship support when she was an undergraduate student. I was tasked with the job of asking her for $5,000 to support student scholarships, and I thought this particular initiative would resonate well with her. At the time, I thought $5,000 was a LOT of money to ask of someone, so, I was shaking in my boots and was intimidated by the thought of meeting her face to face. I find it humorous now, but I made the first error of thinking I could travel to Houston in the middle of the summer with a full suit, tie and all. Well, upon meeting Sue and exchanging the appropriate greetings, she looked me up and down and immediately asked me if I had ever come to Texas in the summer. As beads of sweat and water dripped down my forehead—turns out that there was a torrential downpour on my walk from the parking lot to her office—I nodded embarrassingly and told her that I had not been to Texas during that time of year. She gave me a confirming nod and invited me to take a seat. As I sat in the chair, hot, sweaty, and embarrassed, she immediately tried to relieve me by asking if I wanted to take off my coat.

I recall, as I was taking off my jacket, hearing the sound of my wet and saturated coat unpeel itself from the back of the chair. That unpeeling sound was from all the sticky ironing starch that found a way to quickly adhere to the chair from my clothing. I think Sue heard this sound, but I wasn't sure. At least if she did, she ignored it out of sheer pity. After I gathered my thoughts and took a look down at my waterlogged shoes, I began to have a conversation with her about her experiences as a student. It was a great conversation, and I managed to say all of the right things to Sue, and she seemed to be enthralled by our discussion. The moment of truth came when I had to make the ask. Undaunted by my physical discomfort and being a novice at asking for money, I delivered it. "Sue, I am so happy that your experience as a student was great. You've expressed how the support you received for your education was invaluable, and how it helped to build a strong foundation for your life. Would you be willing to help a bright, deserving student do the same with giving a gift of $5,000 to our fund?" That's it, I put it out there. I let go of all my past beliefs about money and thought about the bigger picture and the impact that her giving could have on future generations of students. This was not about me; it was about them. Sue responded favorably, and for the first time, I realized that I had the power to do some amazing work in this world. I have never looked back since. Although the dollar amounts I solicit now are much higher, I never lose focus on what my role is—to be that vital conduit. You will become more and more comfortable with the idea of asking for money. If you make it about the cause, you will find that your anxiety in doing this type of work will go down tremendously.

The Importance of Enthusiasm

Perhaps one of the most important things that the best people I have seen in this industry have, is a sense of enthusiasm in all that they do. I have learned that the power of enthusiasm is contagious, changing the very nature of the team you work with, your relationships with supervisors, as well as the donors and prospects that you encounter. I'm not talking about this false enthusiasm or a "fake it until you make it" mentality, what I mean is genuine enthusiasm for the many opportunities that have been given to you in life as well as an enthusiasm for being a part of a field that truly makes a difference. Doctors and police officers may save lives throughout the course of their work, but fundraisers play a vital part in preserving life. Being excited about the chance of enhancing or preserving the quality of one's life will motivate you to excel as a fundraiser. As you go about your career, be sure to take the time to reflect and truly look back on all the things that you have accomplished. Outside of the meetings, proposals, and solicitations that you will have to prepare for, think about the effect you are having on the lives your organization serves. This should bring to you this sense of purpose and enthusiasm.

Am I suggesting you bounce around the office with springs on your feet? No, I just mean you should focus on bringing to bear your full attention and energy within the organization you serve. Also, try to approach your work with a sense of gratitude. When I think about all the things that life has given me, coupled with my purpose as a fundraiser, I emerge with this overwhelming sense of peace, happiness, and calm. These thoughts, day in and day out, help to bring a tremendous amount of enthusiasm to all I do. As a fundraiser, you will become excited about the possibility of the things that you can help create through work in philanthropy. If you solely focus just on the money, the gift, or your own personal performance metrics as you go about your work in this business, you will surely be anxiety provoked and panic stricken and at times do things that may not be right for the prospect or the institution. There have been times when I have lost focus on what my job represents and prematurely solicited or rushed a process to get a prospect to give a gift before they were ready. Unless you are lucky, and sometimes it is about luck, these interactions usually don't go favorably. As a fundraiser, you will have an expectation to raise a certain amount of money every fiscal year and will be measured on this, but balance this by properly and systematically planning your prospecting efforts so you are not placed in a state of desperation, which can lead to missteps. Constantly be vigilant about setting visits, identifying new people to fill your pipeline, and planning your solicitations accordingly. Keep your level of activity high on a daily basis. You will find that, through thoughtful and diligent efforts, the numbers you are required to produce, will in fact happen. Lastly, remember that your job is not your life. Always think of the things in your life that you are thankful for—whether it is family, education, health, or the fact that you like to serve the community. Great fundraisers always take a holistic approach to life. I encourage you to do the same.

Know Your Blind Spots

As you grow and learn more as a fundraiser—time and experience will be your biggest allies. While I wish there was a book out there that taught me how to go about my job or perhaps receive a PhD in fundraising, the reality is, in this profession, I had to learn by doing. Given the fact that I did not know much about philanthropy outside of the small efforts my family did for the local church growing up, I had to take what I had learned from my previous professional experiences in my career and translate those over into fundraising. When I first started out, I had many blind spots, and even now I find that every day is in fact a learning experience. In the dynamic world of philanthropy and the intricacies that go along with the psychology of giving, you will be hit by nuances every day. You have to be okay and comfortable with these "blind spots" and know, within yourself, that you possess all you need to do this important work. Your transferable skills will dictate this. In my case, I feel like some of the fundamental principles of my past experiences in sales and in running a small business are parallel to the necessary skill set required to be effective in this profession. Not only is this important, but the ability to be intellectually curious will serve you well. For instance, in this industry, you will work with people who have expertise and interests in a number of subjects from astrophysics to zoology. You have to be comfortable with who you are and know that your ability to ask substantive questions coupled with good active listening skills will make your connections a success. Now, they say ignorance is bliss, so I have a few recommendations for you in the next chapter on how you can in fact be the purveyor of all things. These tips will help you to master the opportunity to chat with the best of them on almost any subject. I do want you to remember that the things you don't know, your blind spots, can in fact be turned into strengths if you always keep an open mind and remain committed to lifelong learning.

Take the Long View

As the saying goes, "You can't see the forest for the trees." It is important for you to know that when you are operating at a high level of fundraising, you have to keep the long view in mind. You will soon learn that fundraising is in fact a long game. Those of you who have been a part of the private sector know the very nature of transactional sales and are probably used to shorter sales cycles. In fundraising, a shorter cycle may work at times for some of the annual level gifts, but when you are working on significant gifts—gifts that can transform the nature of the organization as well as have a tremendous impact on the cause—take a lot more time. A lot of research, conversations, face-to-face meetings, and chances for your prospect to be engaged with your organization are much more commonplace when securing big gifts. This logically makes sense, as a person would not just randomly give their money to an organization they are unfamiliar with. It is a long dating process and it will require you to consciously think of ways that you can creatively engage and involve your prospect—it is truly a long journey. Set the expectation for yourself that bringing in big gifts is a sophisticated process that will take thought, time, strategy, and help from those in your organization. Bringing in a significant gift to an organization will not be just a "you" effort—you will have to rely on certain team members and leadership, and perhaps recruit help from some of your most energized volunteers or board members to make it happen.

Maslow Got It Right

Abraham Maslow was a prominent psychologist who in the 1950s coined the term, "the hierarchy of needs." This theory essentially means that, as humans, we have the ability to thrive and reach our full potential only once our most basic needs have been met. I find that this theory rings true for me and many others I have met in this industry. As you spend your first few years in your organization, you will be clamoring for information, you will be nervous in meetings with donors, and you will, at first, be challenged to find your true identity in your role. However, through the time that you spend experientially learning, meeting with prospects, and becoming more ingrained in your organization, you will develop your "sea legs." In time through constant learning, you will get to a place where you can fully "self-actualize" or operate to your fullest potential as an effective fundraiser. As Maslow mentions, this process may cause some anxiety initially, but over time, as the individual becomes more proficient, a period of higher-level performance is possible. While realizing that Maslow's idea is only one theory among many on the psychology of humans, I think its basic premise holds true. I feel that this will be an important idea for you to consider as you navigate through this world as a fundraiser. In times of self-doubt and insecurity, take heart in the fact that sometimes going through growing pains may be required to help you develop your fundraising muscles. So, don't be discouraged by your blind spots and shortcomings when you first get started. Let them evolve into learning experiences that you will carry with you throughout the rest of your career. Before you know it, you will be at the very top of your field feeling as though you have gotten to a place of true self-actualization.

PART II

CHAPTER 4

Practical and Personal Habits of Highly Effective Fundraisers

Be a Lifelong Learner

You will learn many things in your discussions with your donors and prospects and many times broach subjects that are unfamiliar to you. They will share information with you, whether it be of things that are personal, professional, or perhaps deal with a topical issue that is of utmost importance to them. It is impossible for you to have a depth of knowledge of all the things each and every prospect or donor does professionally, the way they conduct their personal lives, what they read, where they go on vacation, their interest in art or perhaps their love for classical Italian wine. During many of the discussions that I've had with some of my well-traveled prospects, I have found myself giving confirming nods as opposed to responding with substantive information. This was awkward for me and still can be, but I am reassured in the fact that I have committed myself to being better every day and that I have to be comfortable in receiving nuanced information. You must know that there is no way humanly possible for you to know everything that your donors know—otherwise, you would be a walking encyclopedia; however, to hold a conversation with the best of them, commit yourself to lifelong learning to help increase the quality of your interactions. You will also find that the more conversations you have with your prospects, the more you will be able to eventually connect the "informational" dots and perhaps find a common thread woven throughout the nature of all your discussions. There may be certain guideposts within each conversation where you may be able to leverage information from a previous discussion or perhaps from something you have studied or read. So, for instance, if I met with John Smith in Napa Valley, California, and had a discussion with him about varietals indigenous to the region, perhaps what I learned in that discussion I can leverage in my discussion with Nancy in New York when she talks to me about her copious wine collection. This works—you just need to make sure that you are actively listening when you are learning about a subject that is unfamiliar to you, ask open-ended questions, and do your best to read up on a topic that seems unclear to you so that you are able to retain the information. Committing to this principle is a lot of work, but the rewards are exponential. Many times, I found myself picking up the *Wall Street Journal* to read random articles to begin to understand what was going on in the financial sector. Now I have a subscription. I make an effort to attend seminars when I can, read other newspapers and books to see divergent opinions on topics, and listen to podcasts in my car on the way to work or while on a trip. I started to notice that many of the conversations I was having with prospects somehow had some relevance to the articles that I would read and the topics I would study. I pick up books, articles, and magazines on random subjects from finance, economics, and history just to get more perspective on what is going on in the world and feel that I have a stronger appreciation for how things in this world are somehow tied together. This way of learning is completely different from the "regurgitation style" of learning during my high school and early college years where the goal was to simply pass a test. Outside of committing yourself to becoming a lifelong learner, you should be armed with an abundance of information about your organization. This shows that you care about who or what you represent. Knowing the finer points of how your organization serves its mission and where your potential donor might find a connection will be integral to your success in this field. I have noticed that I learn something new every day at work, and I always try to find a practical application of the organization's work so I have a story that I can share with prospects. It is important that you learn how to incorporate the information that you learn and acquire on a daily basis. You can retain most of this information by writing it down and keeping a proper journal of all that you learn. Revisit this often and reflect upon it when you can. Having the feeling of confidence because you have taken the time to learn something that was unfamiliar to you before can be addicting. As your thirst for more knowledge grows deeper, so will your relationships with prospects. This feedback loop will be self-reinforcing, and you will be enthralled by the quality of connections that you are able to make when you commit to consistent learning. The old saying that "knowledge is power" is quite profound. As a lifelong learner, you will develop ideas, plans, and strategic ways of thinking that can really take the nature of how you fundraise to an elevated level. This mindset will allow you to excel at this type of work.

Be Resourceful

Unlike in the days of high school and college when sometimes the answer to a question is staring you right in the face—or in my case located in the back of the book where the answer key is ☺—life as a fundraiser can be ambiguous. You will find that there will not be a simple, cookie-cutter solution in every situation that you encounter. Every donor is different, every organization has a different way of doing things, and applicable laws and procedures with respect to nonprofits may complicate things. You will be asked questions by your prospects or donors that at times you may not be able to answer. For instance, I once had a situation where a donor wanted to give a gift through his estate as well as a cash component to an organization I was working for. Pretty simple right? However, upon further examination, the assets that the donor was looking to bequeath through his estate needed to pass through a long line of beneficiaries. His proposed stipulations required that in order for the organization to receive the gift, this donor and his wife needed to pass away, and that his children— all four of them—needed to be deceased before the organization would eventually receive the money. Coupled with the fact that he was middle-aged himself, this would make it almost impossible for the organization to receive funds for this gift for many years. It was a situation that I was not strongly familiar with, and I had to be resourceful in finding a solution. I had to rely upon the expertise of someone in estate law to help me piece this information together. It turns out that, due to his age and all the contingencies surrounding his children, the organization was unable to accept his commitment. It was a real dissapointment, because of course both he and I wanted this to work, but unfortunately due to timing, it was not possible. Through this experience, I was keenly placed in a position to understand the intricacies of estate law and how philanthropic gifts can be given through insurance policies upon the review of life expectancy actuarial tables. It was unfamiliar territory, but by being resourceful in finding the right information and relying upon the expertise of my colleagues, I was able to navigate through the opportunity. While I would have been happy to accept this gift and pretend that I knew all there is to know, I had the courage to tell the prospect that I needed to rely upon my internal resources to figure all of this out. My point is this, you will run into many nuanced situations throughout the course of your career that will go beyond your capabilities. You have to be okay in knowing this, be upfront with your donor about your lack of expertise in certain areas and rely upon trusted professionals to help you through some of the difficult cases that you will inevitably encounter. Be secure in knowing that it is okay to ask for help and view this as a sign of strength instead of a weakness. Trust me, you will garner more respect by saying you don't know something and doing your research to find out, as opposed to muddling through something you don't quite understand. Good fundraisers don't have all the answers, but they have worked hard to develop the right network of professionals, whether within their organizations or outside, to get the answers that they need in difficult times. I encourage you as you progress throughout your career, to always take the time to build a network of people whose work will complement your work. This investment of time will pay off in the long run and contribute to your professional success. No one can go about the business of fundraising in a vacuum, and I have not come across many people in this industry who have found a tremendous amount of success by going at it alone. Focus on building your network to help enhance your resourcefulness.

Have the Elevator Speech in Check

As you go through the process of finding the organization that is the right fit for you, it will be important for you to be able to articulate the organization's mission well. Do you have to go around repeating an organizational mantra? No, but at any given moment when someone asks you what you do, you should be able to seamlessly rattle off an impactful mission statement about your organization, its priorities, and the role you serve to help complement that mission. If your institution helps to educate underserved children go to college, in a moment's notice, you should be able to have an artful statement at the ready that raises people's eyebrows when you speak. You are doing yourself and the organization a disservice if you present something that is substandard. Believe it, feel it, and exude all of the enthusiasm that you can when you speak about your organization. I mentioned the importance of having enthusiasm in an earlier section, but this, coupled with a well-defined pitch, really packs a punch. Highly effective fundraisers make a habit of always sharpening their pitch, constantly finding ways that they can deliver the vision of their organization. In their articulate, well thought out elevator speeches, they instantly inspire others to take action to either find out more about their organization or perhaps become interested in supporting it. Have you ever seen those Boy Scouts or Girl Scouts out in front of grocery stores or community libraries? These kids innately know the power of a good elevator pitch—one that will get you to act and buy cookies or perhaps that microwave popcorn that you didn't really need. Take the way of the Scouts.

Be Interesting

Highly effective fundraisers by no means have to be stand-up comedians or entertainers. However, having a certain spark about you will speak volumes and help people become more naturally attracted to you. Whether it's the fact that you like to jump out of airplanes, like to feed pre-adopted animals on your weekends, or teach a class in adult education in your free time, these stories can serve you well as you go about your job. As mentioned earlier, I feel that fundraisers are a vital conduit for an organization and when a gift transpires in their relationship with donors it's really not about them; however, being an interesting person can make a difference. The fact of the matter is, no one wants to deal with anyone who has not done "anything." As humans, we are wired and attracted to folks who do interesting things and always are in the mood to hear a good story. As we know, stories really help us to remember things, and as fundraisers, it will be one of the most effective ways that a prospect or donor builds a relationship with you. Stories tend to stick like glue, so make sure your story is an interesting one. Keep your stories vivid, but as a word of caution, avoid stories that may be on controversial topics like religion, politics, or other issues that may be inappropriate for your prospect to hear. Personal struggles should also be off limits as we have to remember our prospects are not our psychologists, so be careful not to "bare your soul." This can make for a very awkward and uncomfortable situation for both you and the person you are meeting with. Remember, as important as it is to be interesting, don't forget the 80/20 rule, where 80% of the conversation you should be focused on actively listening and perhaps the remaining 20%, talking. Your 20% includes the time that may be dedicated to introductory remarks that help build rapport and should include something interesting about you; however, the use of open-ended questions will help you learn more about the prospect's interest.

Speak with Confidence—Dress the Part

In our subjective world, perception is in fact reality. What you say and how you present yourself actually matters. Some of us may have a hard time grappling with this truth and believe that something as superficial as looks are not important. I do think society should view us with a lens that is solely based on who we are at our very core. However, human nature dictates that we are programmed to make judgments on the surface to efficiently process and chunk information into categories that help us make sense of the world. This means that, in our social interactions, we have a tendency to make snap judgments. I have been told that the judgments we make about people happen as fast as 90 seconds upon the encounter. So, when you physically show up, give someone the proper greeting, shake their hand, and begin rapport building, the person across from you has already formed an opinion of who they think you are. I know this may be difficult to take, but, it's true. Finally, know that the impression of who they think you are, sometimes regardless of what future action that you may take to prove otherwise, may be the way in which they will always view you. Right out of the gate, always focus on the impression you want to make when you encounter a prospect or donor—it will leave an indelible mark. Always think and play out the process in your mind; in other words, mentally rehearse how you picture the interaction with your prospect going. You can do a lot to control the perception that people may have of you by visualizing the way you want your meetings to go. You have the power and ability to show up as your highest self—you can look, dress, and accomplish all that you set out to do if you put some effort into it. Set yourself up for success by going into a situation well prepared, ensuring that you are projecting the best representation of who you are. I find that, at the end of the day, every little thing matters when you are dealing with people, and as you continue being the best representation of you and the organization you work for, success and good things will come to you in the process. Your attention to detail and the manner in which you interact with prospects in their eyes, are a reflection of the organization. If you set the right perceptions from the outset, have a strong passion for your organization, and have a confidently well-tuned elevated speech, there is no doubt that you will be on the road to becoming a highly effective fundraiser.

Unconscious Competence

I have been a big fan of many motivational speakers throughout my career and find the work in the arena of personal development to be fascinating. I feel that there are many aspects in fundraising that directly pertain to motivating and influencing others to act, give, or volunteer on behalf of an organization. One of the concepts that motivational speaking really touts is this idea of unconscious competence and one's ability to act "in spite of." Tony Robbins, one of the best motivational speakers in the world, talks about the act of doing things without completely understanding all the nuances and minute details behind taking action. I find that many times we as fundraisers can get bogged down in the details or the weeds of a particular case or prospect, and that we stall before taking any forward-moving action because we have "paralysis by analysis." When we are conflicted about making a decision on what to do with a particular prospect, many times we need to just do the action to get the results we seek. Tony uses the analogy of turning on a light switch. We know when we turn on a light switch that, through the power of electricity, a light will come on. We have the power to turn a light switch on and create light without fully understanding how electricity works on any deeply scientific level. However, we do know that when we reach out our hand toward that switch and take action, results happen. That is the mentality we have to take as fundraisers. Sure, it is important to do your homework on a prospect, and it is important that you meet with all of the internal and external folks who may be able to give you the resources and advice that may be helpful in closing a gift, but at the end of the day, you have to act. You will have to pick up the phone, you will have to send that email, you will have to set that meeting, and you will have to eventually make the ask. If you are stalled in your actions by having to over think and methodically ponder, you will fall short of the true results you seek. I have worked with fundraisers who could literally write a book on some of their prospects because they have gathered so much information, but at the end of the day have never met them. This is because they never took action to set an appointment. Highly effective fundraisers who rely upon unconscious competence know that their skills as a fundraiser and their ability to ask the right questions at the right time, take their performance to unprecedented levels. So be bold, be decisive, and be committed to the principle of unconscious competence. You will be amazed at the results you get when you just take action. Just think in your mind that every substantive step you take, gets you closer to your goal.

CHAPTER 5:

A Donor's Perspective: Highly Effective Fundraisers

I have had the chance to encounter and speak with many donors throughout the course of my many years of fundraising. I have interviewed and gained feedback from actual donors and prospects on what they think makes a highly effective fundraiser, or for that matter what they have witnessed as someone who is highly effective in this industry. Most of the comments that I have gleaned over the years are of a subjective nature. As I mentioned, perception can be reality to some of the people that you will encounter throughout your work as a fundraiser. Below are some representations of conversations that I've had with donors and their opinions about the traits of a highly effective fundraiser. I have purposely kept these conversations anonymous for obvious reasons.

Donor Perspective: "Inspire me"

It can be noted that some of the best in the field have the amazing ability to identify my interests as a donor and somehow always intuitively know how to ask the right questions. Through this open-ended questioning, I feel that I am listened to and heard, and that the fundraiser understands my needs as opposed to throwing a bunch of stuff on the wall and seeing what sticks. The process of questioning takes patience, understanding, and time. I feel that there has to be a strong understanding and level of trust between me and the fundraiser. Sometimes, he or she may ask me to do something that I was not quite ready to do but was compelled to act because it is for the good of the institution. I have noticed that the best fundraisers that I have encountered are highly knowledgeable and take a deep pride in what they do—additionally, they exude enthusiasm and somehow get me fired up about an organization that I may have lost interest in throughout the years. They know how to rekindle that fire. The have a unique power of persuasion and due to their highly infectious attitudes, they inspire me to act. Having a magnetic and dynamic personality goes a long way in influencing me.

Donor Perspective: "It's about me"

We always feel this incredible sense of connectedness when working with a fundraiser who really knows how to handle the ups and downs of the relationship. There are times that require a tremendous amount of patience and understanding when reconciling our philanthropic aims with that of the institution's needs and desires. At times, these things may be in conflict, but a good fundraiser seems to always know how to come to terms with this. Highly effective fundraisers have patience for the long haul and respect how we want to have an impact on their organization. They also truly understand that our philanthropy is a highly personal matter that has to be accomplished on our own timeline. We know that, within every institution, fundraisers have certain metrics that they have to achieve and that their timelines and our timelines may be incongruent. We fully acknowledge this and can appreciate this situation. However, we have found that really good fundraisers balance this pressure effectively by having a comprehensive plan to achieve their goals and have done a good job filling their pipeline with other people to approach for a specific project. This takes the pressure off needing to get a gift from a single prospect. We don't like to feel like we are conducting a transaction when working with a fundraiser who seems to do things in haste in order to "close the deal." We also have noticed something interesting; fundraisers who behave in a transactional nature do not have longevity with the organization. This is sad because in order to build solid relationships with donors and develop strong relationships for the institution, it takes someone who has invested a significant amount of time within the organization. When we are introduced to a new fundraiser, much momentum has been loss, and it is almost like leaving a marriage and going back to the life of dating. An effective fundraiser knows that the most important aspect of their job is the development of the relationship and has a long-term view of how we can have an impact on the organization and its mission. Seeing this big picture and having the vision of what this relationship will look like, not a year from now, but perhaps 5 or 10 years from now, takes a great visionary and someone who is donor centered.

Donor Perspective: "Excite me"

Highly effective fundraisers should be well-versed, well-read, and most importantly, excited about what they do every day. I find this excitement to be contagious and I am compelled by this. I am not talking about jumping head over heels, but a calm and focused excitement about the impact they can have on the organization's mission. I have also noticed how leaders in organizations respect fundraisers that have a true thirst for what they do. These individuals are bold, creative, and unafraid to ask some of the toughest questions. Effective fundraisers excitedly elicit good information from their donors and are influencers who can effect change in an organization. They brilliantly tie the mission and objectives of their organization to what a donor wants to accomplish in their philanthropy. Many times, some of the roads may lead to a dead end as the fundraiser tries to expose the different facets of an organization to potential donors—but they act with vigorous tenacity. The effective fundraisers excitedly and unashamedly go down exploratory paths with their donors and prospects. This may lead to a place that may resonate really well with the prospect or perhaps it won't. However, they are not afraid to reroute, start over, and trust their relationship enough to know that in the long term they will find right things for the donor to also get excited about.

Donor Perspective: An Honest Dealer

Quite frankly, working with a person whose job is to fundraise who has the right values, morals and holds himself or herself to a personal standard is important to me. I think it is important that we get the honest truth about an organization; whether it is about the amount of overhead an organization pays, or the performance of the endowment, a highly effective fundraiser needs to be trustworthy. What I find is that the truth always comes out in the end, so it is best to just be upfront and honest about the workings of the organization. Many times, this true honesty sheds light on where I can have an impact and apprises me on some of the challenges that the organization may face that I may be helpful with. When we get an honest, under-the-hood view of things, it helps focus my efforts on what needs to improve and how I can be helpful. In a way, this actually helps increase my affinity for an organization and helps me in developing the trust in decisions of the leadership within an organization. An organization with a fundraising professional grounded in honesty can only be of benefit to the donor relationship. Organizations that pretend to have it all right give me a sense that they don't really need my help. So, bring on the problems and the honesty!

CHAPTER 6:

Overcoming Daily Challenges and Navigating Politics

Overcoming Daily Challenges

There will be many daily challenges in fundraising—particularly involving establishing and developing true donor relationships. It will be a long and at times, tedious process, but the journey will be rewarding. You will be subjected to the ebbs and flows of this business and the prospect dynamics that go along with it. You will get rejected numerous times and feel the sting of not reaching your designated goals at times. Not to worry, this happens to the best of us, and you have to experience these types of challenges in order to grow better at your craft. You have to have the patience and understanding in knowing that conducting the right activities and applying them consistently will lead you to the results you seek. Please note that it will be those diligent, everyday actions: whether it is making sure that you are consistent in your follow-up communications with prospects or being sure that you are committing time every day to add new folks into your prospecting pool, these actions will lead you to a place where highly effective fundraisers dwell. However, with all of the challenges that you will have while conducting your core activities, you will also have other obstacles.

Politics—Don't Play the Game

You will be challenged daily by the internal pressures of an organization—overly ambitious and sometimes seemingly unrealistic metrics can be a source of tension. Also, when organizations are trying to accomplish many things at a face pace, conflicts can inevitably happen if the overall focus is not clearly understood by everyone. An unfortunate consequence of this lack of clarity and cohesion can have detrimental effects on the staff. Sadly, I have observed and have worked with people who distort the mission of their organization and use it for their own gain or manipulate it for their own political power. This can be dangerous ground, and it is a game that, as a development professional, you don't want to play. In your organization, you will find different organized cultures or subcultures of people—whether they are historically ingrained groups who have always done things a certain way and exercise dominance or perhaps generationally motivated groups who may seem to operate to debunk and demystify the prevailing culture. This is where culture clashes may happen. My candid advice to you if you want to succeed is to make sure that you do not get caught up in this political buzz saw. Always take the high road. Never think you have to play favorites with any particular group to excel in this industry and work hard to build credibility with your colleagues based on mutual and professional respect. If you operate on this level, your status within the organization will be iron clad, and you will not be forced into a situation where the quality of what you do is judged by whom you associate with. As a neutral party, you will be looked upon highly and many times become a mediator when difficult situations arise. Never stoop to anyone's level who is looking to undermine, demean, or set out to tarnish the relationship of another co-worker or development officer. This could lead you down a path of angst and is an unnecessary distraction and problem that you don't need— trust me, your work in the business alone will be challenging enough. So, focus on building great internal relationships with your colleagues, always take the high road, and don't enter a game of politics. These traits, as I have found, will take you high in an organization. I have seen may careers cut short due to politics, and you can simply avoid any potential pitfalls in your career by taking this simple, yet sound advice.

Failures Are Successes

As you have heard the stories of how basketball player Michael Jordan was cut when he first tried out for his high school junior varsity team or how inventor Thomas Edison tried over 1,000 times before he got the light bulb right, many successful people have once walked the road of defeat. Even author of the Harry Potter series, J.K. Rowling, who was essentially homeless, poor, and on welfare, managed to work through her struggles to be one of the best writers the world has ever seen. She was quoted in a famous speech she gave at Harvard University, "It is impossible to live without failing at something, unless you live so cautiously that you might as well not have lived at all—in which case, you've failed by default." You will find that you will learn so much in this industry because of the setbacks and the mistakes that you will inevitably make. As I mentioned earlier, there has not been a definitive, "how to fundraise" manual written—outside of *Fundraising for Dummies*—that will give you a step-by-step guide on how to go about your job. You will have to learn experientially, that is, learn by doing and from those who have been in the fundraising industry for a while. Never underestimate the value of your mistakes, and most importantly, take the time to reflect and learn from them. This seasoning by experiences will in fact come in handy as you begin developing your mental files on what to do when you run across the multiple and sometimes complex scenarios that you will face when fundraising. These stored "experience files" will serve as your own manual as you develop the expertise it takes to navigate through this field. Actor Denzel Washington mentioned in a commencement speech at the University of Pennsylvania, "You will fail, you will look foolish, and you will suck as I have, on your road to success, but the point is that you cannot, by any means, quit." He developed this mentality after going through countless auditions and never landing a role. In the process of scraping your knees and elbows up on this journey, never be afraid to look adversity in the face and embrace it. Remember, you can in fact do all the things that you set out to accomplish and you have to go through tumultuous periods in your career to eventually enjoy a sweet taste of victory—so hang in there. I can recall many days when I would question myself, "What the heck am I doing this for?" or thinking that "this is too hard to endure." What carried me through was my focus on the goals, dreams, and desires of all that I set out to achieve when I originally started. This perseverance has led me to a place of achievement and has made me realize that, as you stick it out, anything can in fact be possible for you.

Scarcity Mentality

I have been known to work with other fundraisers who always seem to come up with excuses as to why they cannot be successful. Instead of looking at and changing their ineffective ways and systems of prospecting, or lack thereof, they blame their lack of success of things such as the stock market when it underperforms, pending legislation adversely affecting charitable deductions, politics, or perhaps that people just don't want to give or don't have the money. All of these are self-projections and excuses that just don't measure up to fundamentally sound development work. We in fact know that wealth is out there. According to the IRS, more than 1.5 million nonprofits are registered in the United States alone. In 2019, more than $449 billion was raised in philanthropic support—one of the highest years on record. Also, we are embarking upon an age where a massive transfer of wealth is occurring—the baby boomers are conducting their estate planning, and as they look to avoid significant estate taxes while providing for their children and grandchildren, we can expect to see significant gifts being made to nonprofit organizations. Many of the 8+ million high-net-worth households in the United States will search for a way to give away their money in order to have an impact on society while they are still alive. During this time—aptly named the Golden Age—several career paths will be positively affected: estate and tax attorneys and—you've guessed it—fundraising professionals. Opportunities clearly exist, it's the scarcity mentality that we need to rid ourselves of. When we shift our thinking to the amount of potential that exists and couple that with sound fundraising work, we can in fact succeed. Never buy into the hype that there are not enough prospects, or not enough opportunities, or that you can't get enough meetings to meet your goals. With some hard work, ingenuity, and creativity—particularly if you form strong relationships with your colleagues and mentors who can help you generate fresh ideas—you will be able to find the prospects and donors who will lead you to the success that you seek. Always approach your job with a positive mentality. Don't be swayed by some of your less than motivated colleagues or by the negative media and news reports. You will be able to find success by staying the course, so approach everything you do in this business with a spirit of abundance and it will in fact come to you.

Culture and Team

In your first 6 months to a year on the job, it is imperative that you work to build the best internal relationships with your colleagues. One of the most important factors that will influence work life is the way you interact with your team and supervisors. As a newcomer to an organization, you will come to notice a certain way in which the team operates based on historical patterns. When joining any new team, you will need to take the necessary time to assess the skills, traits, and personalities of those around you. You should immediately go about identifying people who can be your best resources and advocates and identify and avoid those who exhibit dismissive and negative behavior. Prepare yourself: there will be a few of these negative characters either on your direct team or perhaps across the aisle on another team with whom you may have to work closely. In these situations, be sure to stay true to your values, and as I mentioned in an earlier section, rise above the drama. If you are a new leader to an organization, it is important to take the time to make an honest assessment about what needs to be done to improve the overall performance of your office. A word of caution here: if you are a new leader, always take the time to learn the ins and outs of an organization, its historical way of doing things, and the distinct cultures that may exist. On many occasions, I've seen leaders fail because they come in with the idea that their way of thinking is the best and immediately try to change years upon years of ingrained culture with the hopes that they can turn a huge ship around. The best approach to establishing yourself as a leader is to day-by-day take in the culture, make note of what should be changed, and gather and confer with the right people as you begin to work through ways that can positively make the changes you seek. This approach, as opposed to a "my way or the highway" way of thinking, will minimize the amount of culture clashes and will garner you more respect as a trusted professional. Lastly, this measured approach will help you be more effective in implementing some of the hard changes that many organizations will inevitably have to undergo. What I find is that most organizations that need change are likely to cling to the idea of preserving the status quo. As the saying goes, "No one likes change except a wet baby," so as you progress in your career in fundraising and transition into leadership, place a strong importance on the historical culture, respect it, and find ways to tactfully and gradually make change for the better. The culture and team can be your biggest enemy or greatest ally if you approach both wisely. If you do, you will be revered in your organization.

PART III

CHAPTER 7:

How to Win—The Way Highly Effective Fundraisers Do

Asking for Money

In chapter two of this book, I spoke highly about the value of having a personal philosophy and knowing your "why" as you go about working as a fundraiser for your organization. With a firm belief in the "why" coupled with a firm belief in your organization's mission, making the ask should be considered a natural step in the process. If you have done your due diligence in discovering and learning about a prospect and have taken the time to build a relationship with them over the years, making the ask should be a natural progression in your relationship. The ask is always hard and clunky if the timing is off, the project is off, and the relationship with the donor is fragmented. Cold and untimely asks by their very nature are hard because things are not in sync. As you progress in your career, you will have this intuitive feeling of when the right time is to make the ask. Although I will not take you through the steps of making the ask in this book, there are three things to keep in mind:

Is it the right project? Is it the right donor? Is this the right time to make the ask?

If you stumble in answering these questions, your asks may be misaligned, misdirected or perhaps premature. So, have these components in place before you take the plunge, because after the ask occurs, the very nature of the relationship will change as well—many times for the good if the response is favorable. However, if you find that your ask was not well-received, you will have to go back and rethink your strategy and find a way to make sure that the nature of your relationship with the donor is preserved and that you find ways to get it back on track through more cultivation, relationship building, and information gathering. Also, important in the ask, as was alluded to in chapter five in the donor perspective section, is the idea that the ask is not at all about the fundraiser and his or her priorities, but about the donors and their priorities. Make sure you keep yourself in check and mindful of this concept—that this moment is really not about you and that you play a role as a vital conduit for your organization. When you think on this level and work to make sure that there is a match between the donor's and organization's needs and that fact that you are facilitating this process, it takes some of the pressure off. Of course, the ask is one of the most fun and stimulating parts of the job if you do it right, but keep in mind that if by chance you receive an unfavorable response, by no means should you take it personally. You should remain undeterred and determined in your focus. This resilience will carry you through. So in summary, take the "you" out of the equation, have a commitment to greatness, do your job with the utmost enthusiasm, and remember that your daily efforts have a huge impact on the positive change that we are trying to make in this world. You'd be surprised by how many people will actually be flattered that you have asked and feel privileged about being in the position to give back when we tactfully allow them that privilege. Effective fundraisers get motivated when making the ask because they know every time they do, they are making an impact on an organization's ability to serve their constituents. Making a well thought out ask is a good feeling that you will enjoy repeating in your career.

Active Listening

As I mentioned earlier in this book, your conversations with donors or potential donors will involve asking open-ended questions. Most of the time within your donor meetings should involve them talking and you listening. This is the space that will allow you to really hear their desires, needs, and most importantly, their stories. This involves a skill called active listening, and the best of fundraisers really know how to do it well. I liken this to how a doctor sees a patient and how a diagnosis is given. Most doctors ask their patients what type of symptoms they are having, and most of the times, the patients themselves tell the doctor exactly what's wrong with them. The doctor is then able to prescribe the necessary medication and/or treatment to help their patients. This happens all because the doctor asks questions like, "What brings you in to see me today?". They listen for the response and make the proper diagnosis to ensure their patients take effective action to remedy the problem. Fundraisers do the same. They employ active listening and really hear what's going on in a donor's minds. After a highly effective fundraiser has gathered all of the necessary information and heard all of the things that a potential donor would like to accomplish, they will at that time feel comfortable with prescribing the right "ask." This will be one of your most valuable skills as a fundraiser. Exercise patience with your prospects so you can draw the necessary information out in order to move in a direction conducive to a successful solicitation. With concentrated focus and true listening to the donor's wishes, you will perhaps find that there is a mutual fit in your organization's mission. This is what they call "fundraising magic," and it truly is a wonderful place to be. So, develop your listening muscles and be prepared to exercise this skill in every encounter that you have.

Believe it or not, active listening is hard work, and it requires a tremendous amount of emotional energy. I have noticed after a few donor meetings that I am exhausted, although all I did was sit across from someone and engage them in a discussion. You will at times feel this fatigue at the end of your long days because, again, active listening requires intense focus and this focus requires energy. As a tip, always make sure that you are well-rested the night before you have a donor meeting. Keep your nutrition and hydration in check; otherwise, you will not be able to maintain the focus and the energy that you need to actively listen. Any lack of focus can prohibit you from getting to the place where you can create the fundraising magic that you are hoping to create. Also, if not a distraction to you or the donor, it may behoove you to take notes in case there is some very important information, details, or specifics that you may need later. Some fundraisers I have worked with always go into donor meetings with a notepad, and some find it to be rude and shy away from it. I usually don't take notes until right after the meeting because the information from the conversation is still fresh. I commit myself to writing down important information and any next steps that I need to take so I can be prompt with any necessary follow-up. I have also seen highly effective fundraisers ask for permission to take notes during their meeting with the prospect. Usually, the donor gives a favorable response because they realize that you value what they have to say and how the contents of the conversation may be important to your organization. However, if you find that taking notes distracts your process of active listening, please consider making mental notes as you go along in your conversation. Commit yourself to writing some of the key points of the meeting immediately after. You will be surprised by how much information you retain by writing down key words, names, and phrases that you can later put into a narrative format as you build your prospect file. Shortly written narratives of your conversations with donors will allow you the opportunity to truly think, reflect, and formulate your next steps. This will lead you down a path of success with them. Please note that these thoughts can apply to virtual meetings as well.

Commanding a Room

Highly effective fundraisers have this charismatic aura about them. I realize that this is an intangible skill that not everyone can exude, but there is something magical about an individual who can light up a room. Former President of the United States, Bill Clinton was a master at this. Regardless of whom he spoke to or how big the room he needed to "work", Clinton always had the uncanny ability to connect with anyone at any time and at any place. In a sea of people, he knew how to address an individual in a way that would make them feel as though they were the most important person on the planet at that given time. Bill Clinton had a strong active listening muscle and understood the power of connection. Most people really appreciated this about the former president, and he remains famous for this trait. I have seen some of the best fundraisers have these very same traits. Whether at a public function, gala, small event, or donor meeting, highly effective fundraisers pay keen attention to the individuals they need to connect with and draw people in by their very presence. The aura that they send out establishes a strong connection with others, and by their very nature, these fundraisers command attention in a room. This is the type of person who may or may not be the most extroverted person in the room, but when he or she speaks, people listen. When this person speaks, his or her credibility has been well-established as someone who is great at cultivating personal connections. Their messages resonate soundly not only because of their track record of investing in personal relationships, but also because these highly effective fundraisers make it almost difficult for them to be ignored because of their charisma. I'm not saying that you have to be a Bill Clinton or a Tony Robbins, but you should strive to model the types of behaviors that will gain you credibility among your constituents and colleagues. You can only do this by making a daily habit of constantly focusing on making positive and meaningful interactions with those around you while making sure that you are employing active listening skills. When you are in alignment with how the relationships you build have an effect on the support of your organization, you will be able to speak from the heart in a manner that will be compelling and dynamic. The true power of commanding a room is not the ability to dominate a conversation, but it is the ability to be known as a person who truly cares about the concerns and needs of others while engaging them in a tactful, respectful, and thoughtful manner. Some people consider the ability to relate to others as an aspect of emotional intelligence or EQ. This skill will take time to develop, and you'll have to commit to the process to be highly effective at it. In essence, as you get to the point when you can eventually command a room, captivate an audience and inspire others, know that it truly comes down to being selfless. This is why you decided to get into this industry in the first place. You've realized that this work really is not about you and more about being that vital conduit that can help accomplish some pretty cool things in this world.

A Hyper Focus on the Mission

One of the things that Jim Husson mentioned as I spoke with him about some of the traits that highly effective fundraisers have was their focus on the institution. In chapter two, we talked about the personal connection to the mission that fundraisers should have, but Jim takes it a step further and suggests that the fundraising professional have a "hyper" focus on the institution and its mission. I know that this may seem extreme, but in most cases, when you speak to some of the people who have raised millions and billions of dollars for their organizations, they seem to always possess a few components. They have the necessary experience, trust, and longevity with their organization, and they always act within the organization's best interests. This daily hyper focus on the mission is pervasive in a highly effective fundraiser's interactions, whether internally or externally, as they try to figure out how to best represent their organization. Are they type "A" driven people who never shut off their computers or smart phones? Perhaps, but one thing I do know is that the organization's DNA seems to be in their bloodstream, and they brand themselves as being relentless advocates. I know that this all seems to be really deep, especially if you have never had a feeling like this for anywhere that you have worked, but as you take the time to find the institution that best aligns with your professional and personal passions, perhaps one day you will develop this hyper focus. Hyper-focused fundraisers pay attention to everything that their organization does, who they serve, and the leadership. They constantly contemplate how they can engage donors and prospects to take part in the grand vision of what their organizations are hoping to accomplish. And, these fundraisers tend to measure everything they do by the results that they achieve. You have to be vigilant about the metrics that you hope to achieve with your organization; otherwise, the things you set out to do will not happen. Highly effective fundraisers keep a constant eye on what they are striving to achieve and are not afraid to make the necessary adjustments to attain success. Whether it is raising $100 million or recruiting a diverse set of volunteers for the board, great fundraising professionals constantly monitor their progress and continue to focus on the larger goal at hand. There is a saying that what you focus on expands, so make sure that you are always keeping a watchful eye on all that you are trying to achieve. Again, I know this seems extreme, but taking on the traits of being hyper focused will put you well ahead of the crowd. The fundraising professionals who do not always keep their goals at hand will either simply get lucky or, most of the time, fall short of where they need to be with respect to their professional metrics. So, never be afraid to look under the hood at your activities and make the necessary adjustments if you find yourself wandering off course. This will help you become hyper focused.

Self-Motivated and Goal Oriented

This goes without saying, but as you gleaned from earlier chapters, highly effective fundraisers are always self-motivated and employ goal setting in their professional and personal lives. You must constantly ask yourself, "What do I want to achieve in my career?", "What do I have to accomplish in my role now to be successful in my long-term goals?" and "What are the most important skills I need to develop to be better at what I do?". This reflective thinking and constant self-assessment will help you always look at the big picture and bring more clarity to all that you are trying to achieve. As Zig Ziglar, the famous motivational speaker, author, and unrivaled salesperson would say, "How can you hit a target that you cannot see?" You should always have your goals on prominent display as well as embedded in your mind. I would employ the art of visualization and see yourself in the career, position, or specific achievement you aspire to attain. Make a daily habit of writing down the things that you need to accomplish to reach your short-term goals—this will help you make an honest effort in staying on track. Celebrate the wins, whether they be small or large, and reflect upon what you did to get the results that you achieved. Learning from your experiences, whether positive or negative, is in and of itself, success. Regarding long-term goals, think about that big, audacious dream you have for yourself, your career, and your family. Make sure that these things are all in alignment with each other, because if they are out of alignment, the universe can't bring you the holistic success that you seek. Always take these things into account when creating an action plan and when creating big, long term goals. As a highly effective fundraiser attains success and gets closer and closer to his or her goals, a momentum develops that perpetuates this cycle. Whether it's closing big gifts or rising to the ranks of management, achievement fuels the motivation of an individual to continue to reach their goals in a successive manner. Don't forget to look for the small wins as well—they will always lead to bigger ones. Remember that taking steps, in either direction are still steps, and I have come to learn that at times, sheer motion itself creates a result.

CHAPTER 8:

Emerging as a Leader in Fundraising

You will find that, as you read through some of the advice in this book and develop the habits of a highly effective fundraiser, there will be a plethora of good opportunities that will come your way. These opportunities can come in the way of promotions and other allowable incentives. Additionally, you may be highly recruited to join good organizations who want to make your career change worthwhile. I have seen people in this industry who make for very good fundraisers and have a natural and keen ability to do well. These dynamic individuals have a knack and a gift to fundraise at the highest of levels and are renowned for their uncanny ability to help transform organizations due to the tremendous amount of money that they have raised. You are reading this book because someday this will be you and you will have to make the choice whether you will want to rise to the ranks of managing people and teams or if you would be better suited to remain on the front-line as a so-called "rainmaker." I am not here to tell you which choice would be best for your own skill set and personality, but I can tell you that taking on a leadership or a management role in an organization is not a responsibility that can be taken lightly; nor does one's heralded success in fundraising equate to being a good manager.

Be There for Your People

If you decide that you are cut out for management and see your-self as a leader within the organization, not only should you have a track record of success, a mentality that is selfless, but you'll also need to be relentlessly focused on the people who will be serving. That's right, management and leadership involve YOU being the servant. Management theorists, Robert Greenleaf wrote extensively on how managers and leaders are called upon to make sure the needs and priorities of those they manage are foremost. Greenleaf argues that only after intensely focusing on the needs of others, can one aspire to become a great leader. This seems contradictory to many who believe in the traditional model of management where the leader's word is the order of the day. Some of the basic tenets of servant leadership also include the follow-ing: listening, empathy, healing, awareness, persuasion, and a commitment to growth of your people. I believe these qualities

are possessed by some of the best leaders that I have seen in organizations; however, these individuals are hard to come by because
of the autocratic nature of the position itself. In the eyes of the
wrong person, the label of manager may connote a master/subor-
dinate paradigm that may unfortunately lead to the exploitation of
employees. I have observed managers who promote undermining
and manipulative behaviors over the very people they are there
to support. This creates a culture of dysfunction and distrust that
would be appalling to most donors if they knew about it. However,
as the servant leader, you will do things differently. With a genuine respect and care for the best interests of your people, you will
make decisions that at times may be difficult for you as a leader,
but work for the best of the organization and the people within it.
These leaders fully acknowledge the responsibility they have and
manage to the best of their ability, realizing that it is "not about
them." The servant manager is always there for the employees
and has worked hard to build the internal credibility and respect
from those around him or her to make decisions for the greater
good. Remember these things when you are called upon to lead!

Model the Behavior that You Want to Encourage

During the time that I served in the Marine Corps, I learned
a very important and valuable lesson on leadership. One of the

things that I noticed as I left the enlisted ranks and went to Officer Candidate School in Quantico, Virginia, was the fact the Marines I would later lead, came to admire and respect my role in a notable way. The men in my platoon knew I truly understood their mentality and had the ability to relate to them in ways through having a shared connection. I also noticed that Marines were more ready to do things and be more inspired by a leader who did things in the same manner in which they did. In other words, they felt that because I had gone through some of the same struggles and challenges and have "walked in their shoes" in the enlisted ranks, I could empathize with them. They had the confidence in knowing that they can take direction from someone who has been there and done that. You will find throughout your career leaders and managers who embrace servant leadership and always do things for the benefit of the team because they truly have had the right connecting experiences. They have been in the trenches and teach what they know because of their experiences. When called upon, these leaders are prepared at any given moment to roll up their sleeves and do the work necessary to accomplish a mission. I have noticed some of the best leaders in the development world have spent years gaining the relevant experience to lead a team. The lessons learned from their experiences set a formidable example and model for their respective teams and sends a signal of competence. I have been known to lead and inspire teams to act simply because they know that, at any given moment, I would do what I ask them to do. They know this, and it motivates them to do great things. So as you become a leader in your organization from the years of gathering a tremendous amount of know-how, be cognizant of the fact that the people around you are watching your actions and will model the behavior that you display. As a leader, you will have to hold yourself to a higher standard and be willing to do what is necessary to get your team in motion. To this day, although I have a tremendous administrative workload in managing people and teams, I still stay true to my roots as a fundraiser and remain diligent in my prospecting actions. I am still effective as a fundraiser because I give constant focus to the daily activity it takes to be a successful. My peers, colleagues, and respective team members see that this juggling of responsibilities takes enthusiasm, organization, and passion and are inspired themselves to take action. Never forget your roots as a fundraiser and never get out of the practice of the actual business of fundraising—it's almost like anything else: if you stop doing it, you will get out of the habit and your skills will become dull. So stay positive, work hard, and be committed to leadership by example.

The Culture of Success

If you focus on being a servant leader and are committed to your team, your profession, and your craft, you will create a culture of success. As I mentioned before, it takes time to affect change in the work place, so you have to focus on this daily while also respecting the history of what your organization's culture has been. Gradually over time you will start to see some positive changes, but you must remain steadfast and undeterred in your thoughts, actions, and behaviors. Don't be afraid to set the example, and certainly do not be afraid to get your hands dirty. People will look to you for guidance, and you have to be there for them with solid and confidently spoken advice that is based not only on your experiences, but also on taking a realistic look at what needs to be done. A culture of success is created by a team who feels that they can take action because their leader supports them, with accountability and commitment shared on both sides of the equation. Upfront and honest communication helps to facilitate this. I have seen the opposite effect happen, one in which people work in fear and are afraid to act because of a culture of distrust. Management theorist and author Patrick Lencioni keenly talks about this in his book *The Five Dysfunctions of a Team*, where he points out some of the breakdowns in team performance. The first of the five is a sheer lack of trust—distrust of the leader and his ability to lead competently, lack of trust that one can express an opinion freely, and lack of trust in the overall direction of the team and its goals. These breakdowns are detrimental, particularly for leaders who have not championed the ideas of servant leadership and have not demonstrated to his or her team that they are a competent professional. As you demonstrate your

LAUNCHING A CAREER IN PHILANTHROPY

capabilities to your team, keep in mind one of the most powerful
things that you can ever do: build a strong foundation upon trust
and respect. Then and only then can you truly achieve the culture
of success that you seek.

The Money Will Follow You

When you do a great job in this industry, as my idol Geoffrey
Canada wrote to me in a letter, "rich rewards will come." Contrary
to what you hear about this industry not being lucrative, the fundraising profession itself is one of the top industries that you can
be in right now. I will go through some of this in the next chapter,
but I have to say that there are many opportunities to not only
do social good but also make a handsome living and abundantly
provide for you and your family. What we are finding is that
fundraising jobs are in high demand, and as the generational
wealth transfer occurs, there will be a few careers that will be
highly coveted. You've guessed it, this is one of them. You may
be initially discouraged with the salary when you go into your
first fundraising job, but like all things, good things come to
those who wait. I recall when I made the switch to the nonprofit
world because I had a personal passion to do so but realized that
the compensation wasn't what I thought it would be. I willingly
immersed myself into the field with the hopes that one day it
would pay off financially. I can now honestly say that making the

choice to join this industry has paid off in so many ways and has broadened my career in ways that I never thought were initially possible. It could be the same for you, but you must stick with it. A close colleague of mine said the following, "Do the hard work that is required of you, don't focus so much on the money and it will come." This has served me well because I have noticed that great things happen to people who truly commit themselves to this and focus on doing the best job that they can possibly do. Also contrary to popular belief, fundraisers are not professional beggars who live meager lives. They are people who work for the very best of institutions and organizations. They create positive and lasting change and are paid well because of their ability to inspire and lead. Additionally, they exhibit their perseverance by possessing an undying spirit of winning. These folks do very well and put themselves on a path not only to achieve professional success but also to enjoy a comfortable lifestyle that working in this industry allows. The sky's the limit!

CHAPTER 9:

New to the Field? Insights on How to Make Your New Career in Fundraising Happen!

Contemplating This Career?

Many of you are in the midst of doing some soul-searching on what your next career move may be. There are some encouraging signals out there. As I mentioned, there are more than 1.5 million nonprofits in the United States alone and in 2019, more than $449 billion was raised in philanthropic support. In my conversations with industry recruiters, I have learned that at least eight jobs exist for every marketable fundraiser. So, don't worry if you don't have that PhD or JD—you can still lead a successful and prosperous career. If you do have these advanced degrees and work in the development world, this will benefit you greatly. As organizations seek to maximize their outreach and find creative ways to raise funds for their respective missions, the call for competent fundraising professionals is loud and clear.

Perhaps with your current skill set, you can answer this call.

As I reflect upon my time spent reviewing stacks and stacks of resumes during my years in the nonprofit sector, I have noticed that many candidates possess the relevant fundraising and development experience, but many also possess highly relevant transferable skills. These candidates hail from such industries as banking and finance, retail, business development, and B2B sales. Job seekers who have a background in sales and marketing, entrepreneurial pursuits, and consulting are providing a strong benefit to the nonprofit industry. This professional diversity has complemented the sector well. The good news is: you don't have to show a track record of having raised millions of dollars before securing a job as a fundraiser, but you should have some fundamental relationship-building skills and the ability to understand the process of identifying potential donors for an organization. Many prospects have a natural affiliation with the organization that makes outreach easier. For instance, for an institution of higher education, the natural prospecting base would be the alumni; for a museum or arts organization, it would be their patrons; for a hospital, it would be the grateful patients, and so on. For those of you who are used to cold-calling and picking up the phones to try to get appointments with complete strangers—the nonprofit industry gives you an advantage of knowing that the person you are trying to engage at the very least has or has had some interest in the organization. So, I would argue that the calls that you make are actually "warm" calls—I have a training designated for the method of conducting outreach and "cold calls" in the nonprofit industry that I am happy to share.

HELPFUL TIPS

Here are a few tips to help you get started on the path to becoming a highly effective fundraiser:

1. Develop a compelling story or personal reason as to why you are looking to join a specific organization. You will most likely have to tell this story to your interviewers and donors, as they will want to know your level of interest and passion for joining the organization. Also, having this in check will make your job a lot easier.

2. Boost your resume and exposure in this industry by joining organizations such as the Association for Healthcare Philanthropy (AHP) or your local Association of Fundraising Professionals Chapter (AFP) or the Council for Advancement and Support of Education (CASE)—some of their programming can be very helpful as you learn about the nonprofit sector.

3. If you currently work at a nonprofit, ask whether you can take on some fundraising responsibilities. Perhaps there may be some opportunities to help with some of the smaller solicitations like phone calls or mailings that go out to potential prospects.

4. Volunteer for an organization similar to the one you wish to join. This most likely won't be a paid opportunity, but it will help you gain some necessary experience as well as give you a taste of what working for that organization is like.

5. Shadow for a day—some organizations may allow you to do this or perhaps allow you to undertake an internship opportunity. You never know—this could eventually evolve into an opportunity for you.

6. Take courses—programs may be offered in your community or perhaps online—in which you can educate yourself about the nonprofit industry. Understanding topics such as the legal ramifications of a 501c3 and what an endowment is will be helpful in advancing your career.

7. Talk to trusted professionals who are already doing great work in this field. I can't remember how many informational interviews, coffees, and conversations I have had when I was first contemplating entering this field. Having the right mentor was key for me and was also helpful when the time came for me to interview.

8. Take inventory of your transferable skills and be prepared to showcase them and how they are parallel to the job you seek. If you have worked with wealthy clients at a major bank, specifically on wealth advising, be sure to highlight this in your conversations.

Lastly, always remember, "Stay on this path—it will bring you rich rewards." I encourage you to explore, learn, and stay on the path of maximizing the skills that you have accumulated and use them for the greater good of humanity. Now go out and be the change that you hope to create!

CONTACT ME

Thank you for taking the time to read this book. I hope it helps as you embark upon this precious journey. Feel free to contact me at harveygreen501@gmail.com should you ever have any questions, or just want to talk through anything fundraising related.

Wishing you much success!

Sincerely,

Harvey